BIRDS

BIRDS

DOVERPICTURA

DOVER PUBLICATIONS, INC. | Mineola, New York

GREEN EDITION ®

At Dover Publications we're committed to producing books in an earth-friendly manner and to helping our customers make greener choices.

Manufacturing books in the United States ensures compliance with strict environmental laws and eliminates the need for international freight shipping, a major contributor to global air pollution. And printing on recycled paper helps minimize our consumption of trees, water and fossil fuels.

The text of this book was printed on paper made with 10% post-consumer waste and the cover was printed on paper made with 10% post-consumer waste. At Dover, we use Environmental Defense's Paper Calculator to measure the benefits of these choices, including: the number of trees saved, gallons of water conserved, as well as air emissions and solid waste eliminated.

Courier Corporation, the manufacturer of this book, owns the Green Edition Trademark.

Please visit the product page for *Birds* at www.doverpublications.com to see a detailed account of the environmental savings we've achieved over the life of this book.

By Alan Weller.
Designed by Juliana Trotta.

Birds is a new work, first published by Dover Publications, Inc. in 2011.

The CD-ROM file names correspond to the images in the book. All of the artwork stored on the CD-ROM can be imported directly into a wide range of design and word-processing programs on either Windows or Macintosh platforms. No further installation is necessary.

ISBN 10: 0-486-99158-X
ISBN 13: 978-0-486-99158-0

Manufactured in the United States of America by Courier Corporation
99158X01
www.doverpublications.com

STORK

008

007

009

010

background 012

011

013

014

11

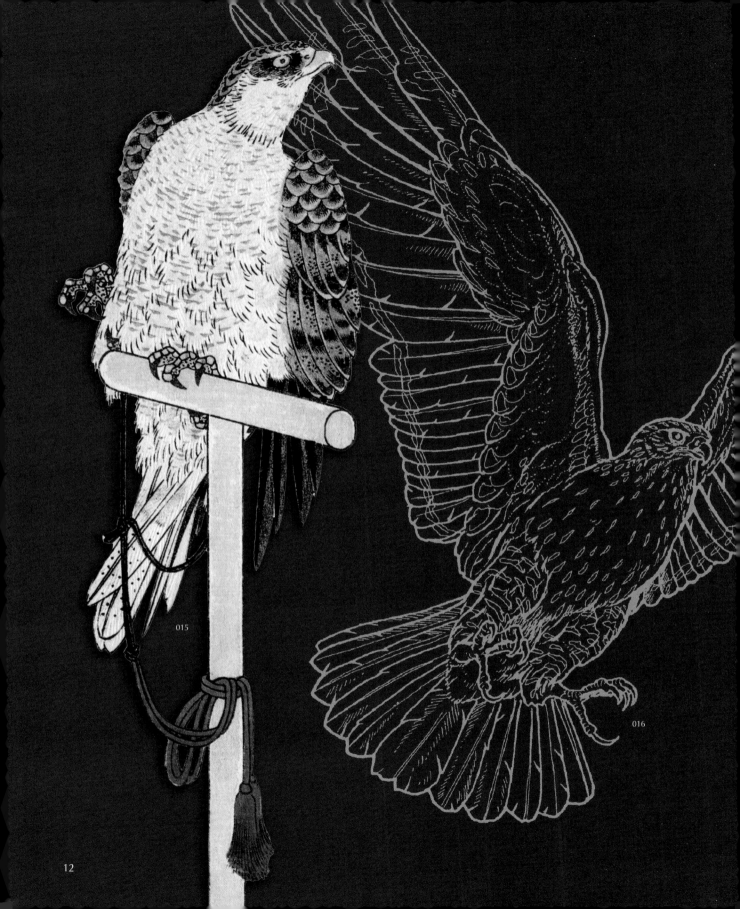

015

016

019

background 020

021

022

023

025

026

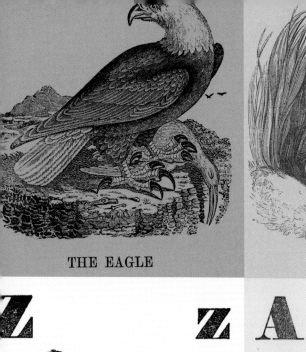

THE EAGLE

THE IBIS.

THE BLUE BIRD.

Z z

THE LETTER Z, OR ROOST.

A

a

THE AUK.

T

THE TURKEY.

F f

H h

Q

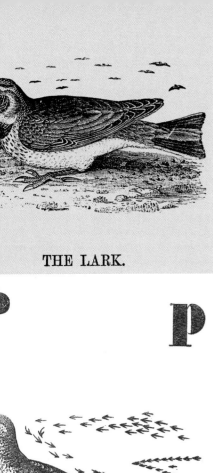

THE LARK.

THE SWALLOW

THE GOOSE.

p

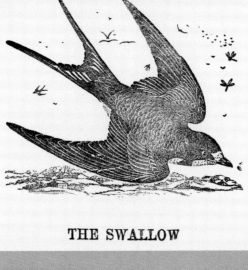

V

v R r

THE PIGEON

THE VULTURE.

THE ROBIN.

J u K k J j

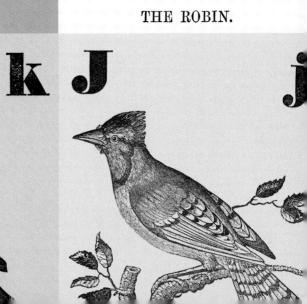

- 044

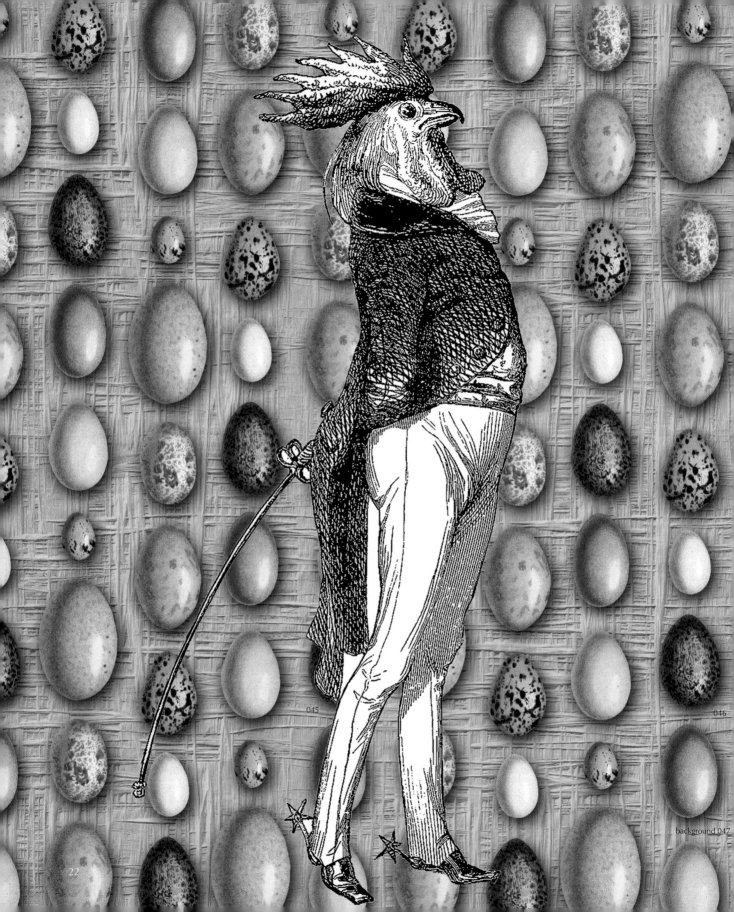

045

046

background 047

049

051

052

background 053

054

055

background 056

background 058

057

29

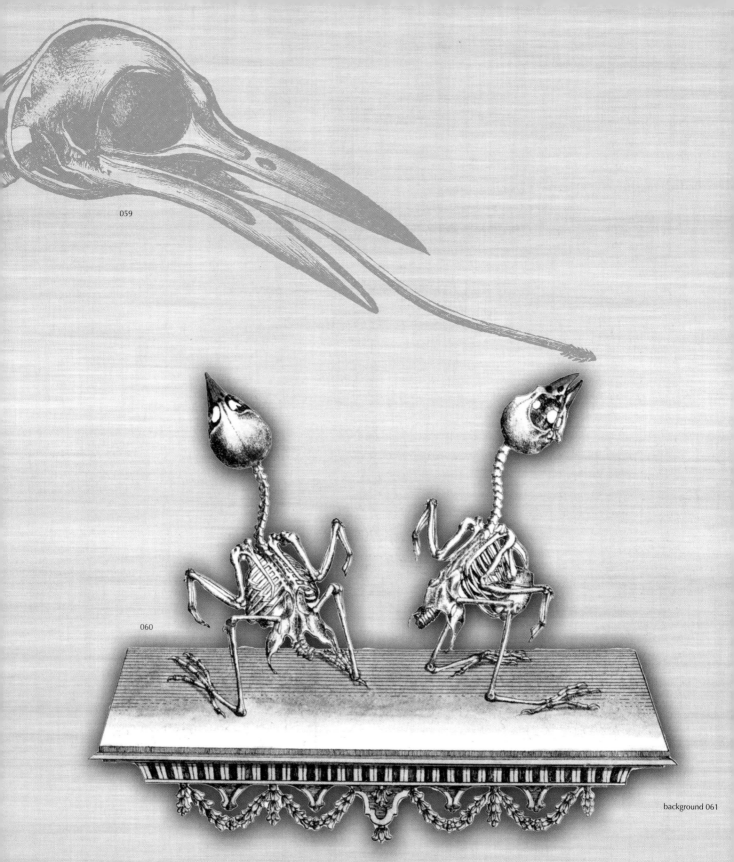

059

060

background 061

30

062

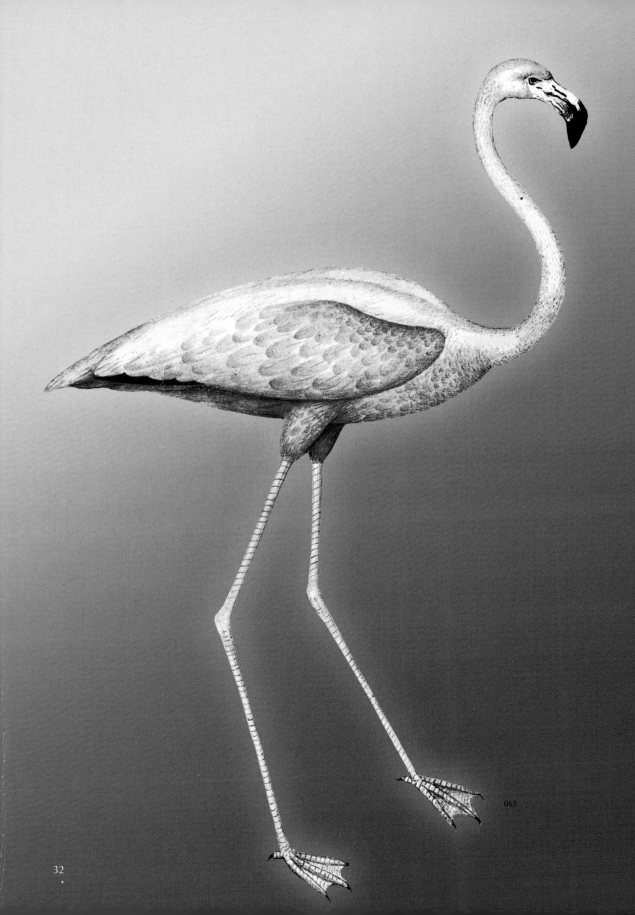

063

064

067

background 068

background 070

069

37

071

072

073

background 074

075

076

077

078

079

080

081

083

085

086

084

087

088

089

090

091

092

48

093

094

096

097

098

099

100

101

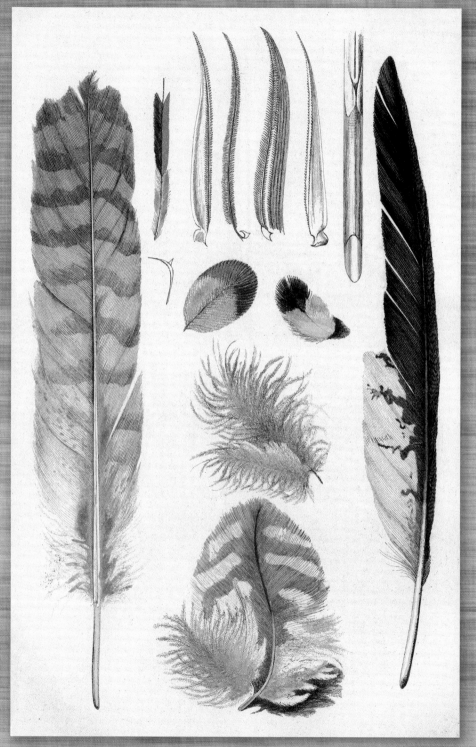

102

105

106

107

108

58

60

110

111

114

113

background 115

62

116

117

120

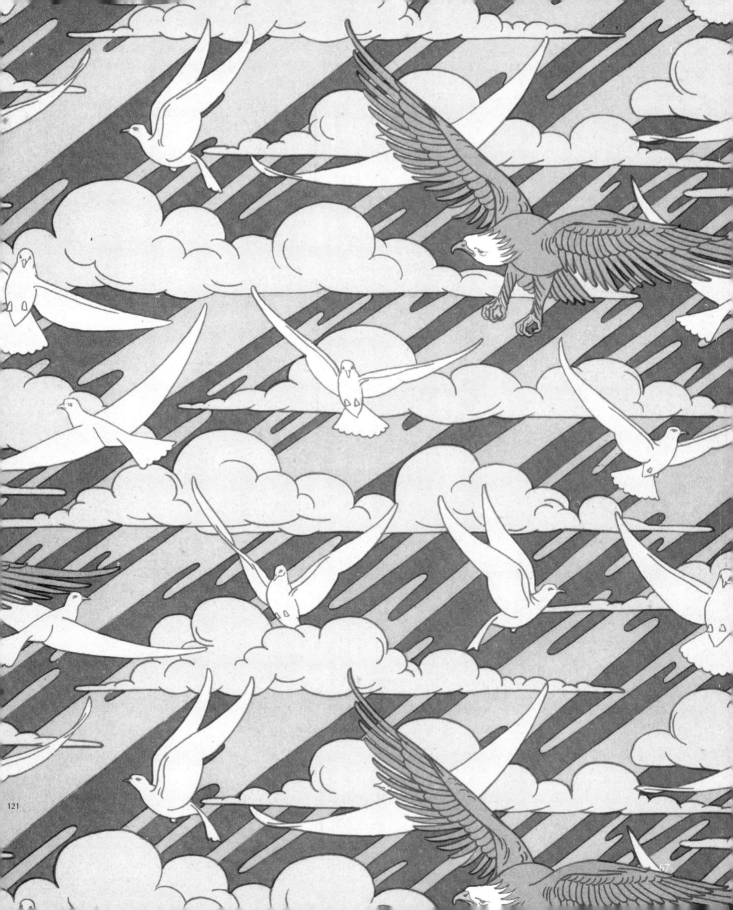

background 126

125

69

127

128

130

131

134

135

136

137

138

139

140

141

142

143

144

145

146

147

148

149

150

151

152

153

155

156

88

background 160

159

161

162

163

164

background 165

166

background 167

168

background 169

173

174

175

background 176

177

179

180

background 181

104

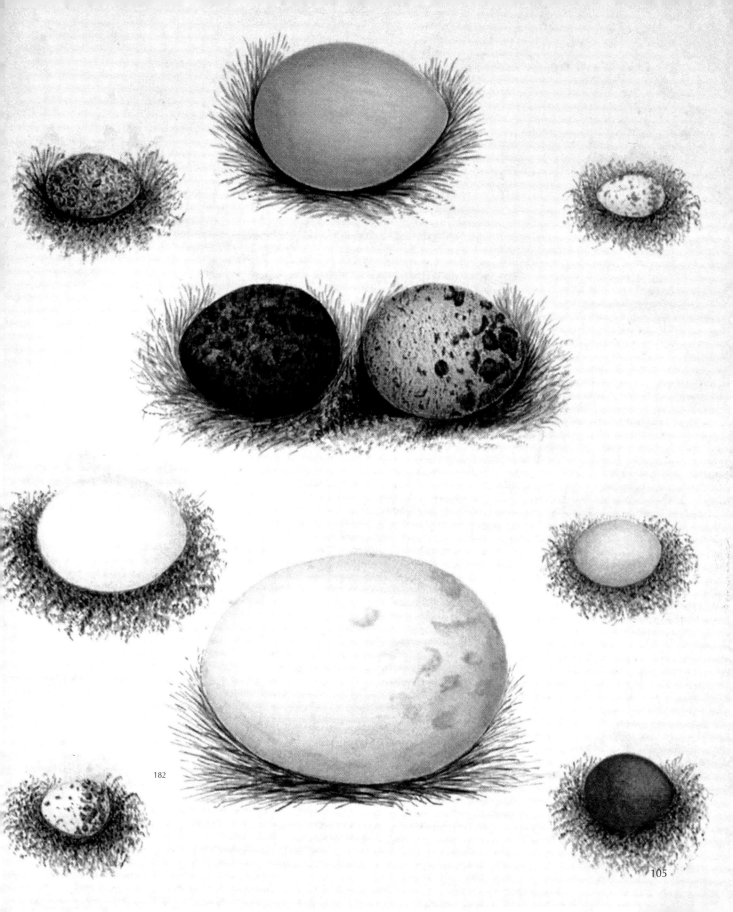

182

183

185

background 186

108

187

background 188

109

189

110

190

LE GEANT.

191

192

LE SOLITAIRE

193

194

background 195

114

196

198

199

background 200

201

202

P

O

N

M
L

K
J

I

203

H G F E D C B A

background 206

207

208

209

210

211

212

background 213

214

background 215